Healthy Choices

STAYING ACTIVE AND EXERCISING

By Kristen Susienka

New York

Published in 2022 by Cavendish Square Publishing, LLC
243 5th Avenue, Suite 136, New York, NY 10016

Copyright © 2022 by Cavendish Square Publishing, LLC

First Edition

No part of this publication may be reproduced, stored in a retrieval system, or transmitted in any form or by any means—electronic, mechanical, photocopying, recording, or otherwise—without the prior permission of the copyright owner. Request for permission should be addressed to Permissions, Cavendish Square Publishing, 243 5th Avenue, Suite 136, New York, NY 10016. Tel (877) 980-4450; fax (877) 980-4454.

Website: cavendishsq.com

This publication represents the opinions and views of the author based on his or her personal experience, knowledge, and research. The information in this book serves as a general guide only. The author and publisher have used their best efforts in preparing this book and disclaim liability rising directly or indirectly from the use and application of this book.

All websites were available and accurate when this book was sent to press.

Library of Congress Cataloging-in-Publication Data

Names: Susienka, Kristen, author.
Title: Staying active and exercising / Kristen Susienka.
Description: New York : Cavendish Square Publishing, 2022. | Series: Healthy choices | Includes index.
Identifiers: LCCN 2020030980 | ISBN 9781502659569 (library binding) | ISBN 9781502659545 (paperback) | ISBN 9781502659552 (set) | ISBN 9781502659576 (ebook)
Subjects: LCSH: Exercise–Juvenile literature. | Physical fitness–Juvenile literature.
Classification: LCC RA781 .S887 2022 | DDC 613.7/1–dc23
LC record available at https://lccn.loc.gov/2020030980

Editor: Greg Roza
Designer: Andrea Davison-Bartolotta

The photographs in this book are used by permission and through the courtesy of: Cover wavebreakmedia/Shutterstock.com; p. 5 Ty Allison/Photographer's Choice/Getty Images Plus/Getty Images; p. 7 SDI Productions/iStock/Getty Images Plus/Getty Images; p. 9 monkeybusinessimages/iStock/Getty Images Plus/Getty Images; pp. 11, 17 FatCamera/E+/Getty Images; p. 13 SDI Productions/E+/Getty Images; p. 15 skynesher/E+/Getty Images; p. 19 (left) Pixel_Pig/E+/Getty Images; p. 19 (top right) kali9/E+/Getty Images; p. 19 (bottom right) Robyn Beck/AFP via Getty Images; p. 21 HRAUN/E+/Getty Images; p. 23 Jose Luis Pelaez Inc/DigitalVision/Getty Images.

Some of the images in this book illustrate individuals who are models. The depictions do not imply actual situations or events.

CPSIA compliance information: Batch #CW22CSQ: For further information contact Cavendish Square Publishing LLC, New York, New York, at 1-877-980-4450.

Printed in the United States of America

CONTENTS

Get Moving!	4
How Exercise Helps You	8
Different Ways to Stay Active	14
Words to Know	24
Index	24

Get Moving!

Healthy people take good care of their body. One important way they do this is by moving their body. Exercising and staying **active** are big parts of living a healthy life. Exercise can also be a lot of fun!

It's good to be active every day. Kids should spend at least an hour every day doing some kind of **physical** activity. This helps them grow up strong and healthy.

7

How Exercise Helps You

Exercise helps different parts of your body. Many exercises make your heart beat faster. They can also make you breathe harder. This helps your heart and **lungs** get stronger. Running helps your heart and lungs.

You can also do different exercises to make different **muscles** stronger. Dancing can help make your leg muscles stronger. Lifting weights can help make your arm muscles stronger. Learning how to lift weights safely is important!

Staying active is good for your mind too. It can help you feel happier when you're sad or angry. It can also help people who feel anxious, or nervous and afraid. If you feel down, try moving around!

Different Ways to Stay Active

Some people go to a gym to stay active. Others go to exercise classes. These are good ways to get moving, but you can do other activities too. Walking with your family is a great way to exercise!

Swimming is another fun way to stay active. When you swim, you use many different muscles at the same time. You also help your heart and lungs stay healthy. You can swim on a team or just for fun!

Playing sports is a great way to get moving! You can join a baseball or softball team. You can play soccer for your town. You can even play football in your backyard or at a park.

19

Yoga is a kind of exercise for the body and the mind. You put your body in different yoga poses, or shapes. You also breathe deeply. This can help you feel better if you're feeling anxious or sad.

21

Everyone exercises differently. Some people run. Others ride their bike. Some people play basketball. Others dance around their house. It doesn't matter how you move.
All that matters is you keep moving!

WORDS TO KNOW

active: Doing things that call for a lot of movement.

lungs: Body parts that take in air when a person breathes.

muscles: Body parts that allow a person to move.

physical: Having to do with the body.

INDEX

H
heart, 8, 16

L
lungs, 8, 16

M
mind, 12, 20

muscles, 10, 16

R
running, 8, 22

S
sports, 18

swimming, 16

Y
yoga, 20